piano ★ vocal ★ guitar

best of IGGY POP

ISBN 978-1-4234-8200-0

HAL•LEONARD® CORPORATION
7777 W. BLUEMOUND RD. P.O. BOX 13819 MILWAUKEE, WI 53213

Visit Hal Leonard Online at
www.halleonard.com

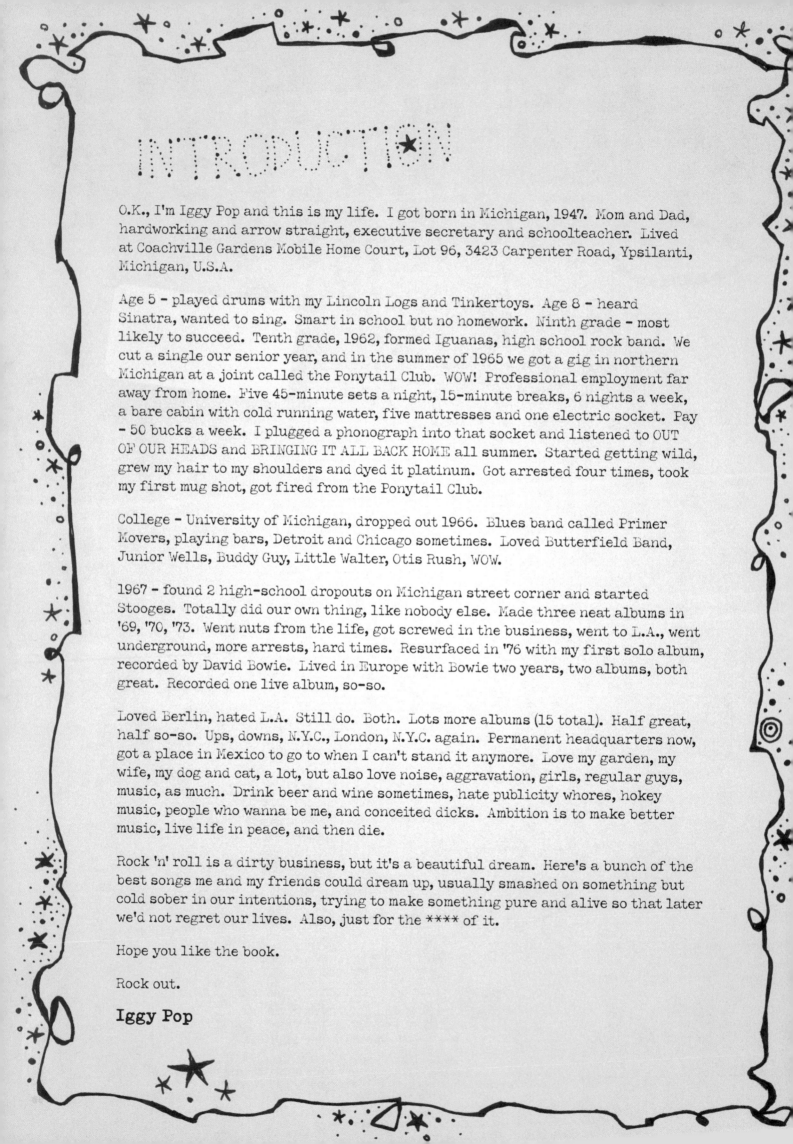

INTRODUCTION

O.K., I'm Iggy Pop and this is my life. I got born in Michigan, 1947. Mom and Dad, hardworking and arrow straight, executive secretary and schoolteacher. Lived at Coachville Gardens Mobile Home Court, Lot 96, 3423 Carpenter Road, Ypsilanti, Michigan, U.S.A.

Age 5 - played drums with my Lincoln Logs and Tinkertoys. Age 8 - heard Sinatra, wanted to sing. Smart in school but no homework. Ninth grade - most likely to succeed. Tenth grade, 1962, formed Iguanas, high school rock band. We cut a single our senior year, and in the summer of 1965 we got a gig in northern Michigan at a joint called the Ponytail Club. WOW! Professional employment far away from home. Five 45-minute sets a night, 15-minute breaks, 6 nights a week, a bare cabin with cold running water, five mattresses and one electric socket. Pay - 50 bucks a week. I plugged a phonograph into that socket and listened to OUT OF OUR HEADS and BRINGING IT ALL BACK HOME all summer. Started getting wild, grew my hair to my shoulders and dyed it platinum. Got arrested four times, took my first mug shot, got fired from the Ponytail Club.

College - University of Michigan, dropped out 1966. Blues band called Primer Movers, playing bars, Detroit and Chicago sometimes. Loved Butterfield Band, Junior Wells, Buddy Guy, Little Walter, Otis Rush, WOW.

1967 - found 2 high-school dropouts on Michigan street corner and started Stooges. Totally did our own thing, like nobody else. Made three neat albums in '69, '70, '73. Went nuts from the life, got screwed in the business, went to L.A., went underground, more arrests, hard times. Resurfaced in '76 with my first solo album, recorded by David Bowie. Lived in Europe with Bowie two years, two albums, both great. Recorded one live album, so-so.

Loved Berlin, hated L.A. Still do. Both. Lots more albums (15 total). Half great, half so-so. Ups, downs, N.Y.C., London, N.Y.C. again. Permanent headquarters now, got a place in Mexico to go to when I can't stand it anymore. Love my garden, my wife, my dog and cat, a lot, but also love noise, aggravation, girls, regular guys, music, as much. Drink beer and wine sometimes, hate publicity whores, hokey music, people who wanna be me, and conceited dicks. Ambition is to make better music, live life in peace, and then die.

Rock 'n' roll is a dirty business, but it's a beautiful dream. Here's a bunch of the best songs me and my friends could dream up, usually smashed on something but cold sober in our intentions, trying to make something pure and alive so that later we'd not regret our lives. Also, just for the **** of it.

Hope you like the book.

Rock out.

Iggy Pop

BEST OF IGGY POP

BANG BANG

Written by IGGY POP
and IVAN KRAL

CANDY

Written by
IGGY POP

All my life ___ you're haunt-ing me, ___ I loved you so. ___ Can - dy, Can - dy, Can - dy, I ___ can't let you go. ___ Life is cra - zy. ___

Repeat and Fade

BUTT TOWN

Written by
IGGY POP

CHINA GIRL

Written by IGGY POP
and DAVID BOWIE

She says: "shhh" ____

she says: "shhh." ____

Oh, oh, oh, oh, oh, ____ lit - tle Chi - na girl.

Repeat and Fade

COLD METAL

Written by
IGGY POP

CRY FOR LOVE

Written by IGGY POP
and STEVE JONES

Lyrics:
Sta - tus seek - ers __ I nev - er cared __
Bad __ T V that __ in - sults me free - ly; __

Instrumental solo

NIGHTCLUBBING

Written by IGGY POP
and DAVID BOWIE

Moderately slow shuffle

Night-club-bing,   we're night-club-bing,   oh, is-n't it wild? ___
night-club-bing,   bright white club-bing.   Oh, is-n't it wild? ___

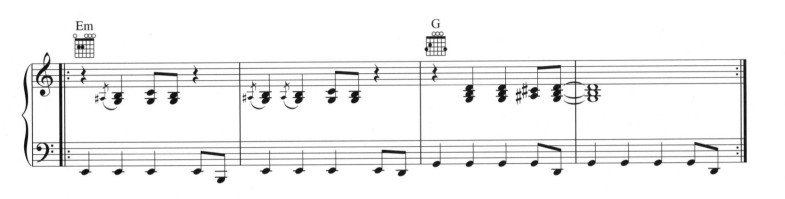

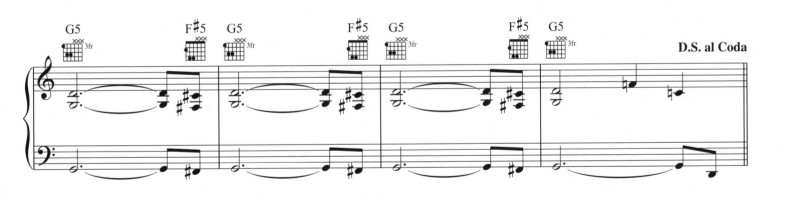

FIVE FOOT ONE

Written by
IGGY POP

Bright Rock

Play 3 times

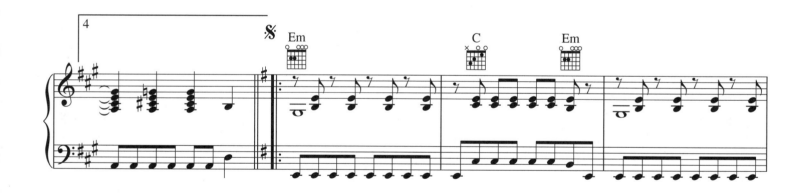

I'm on-ly five-foot - one.

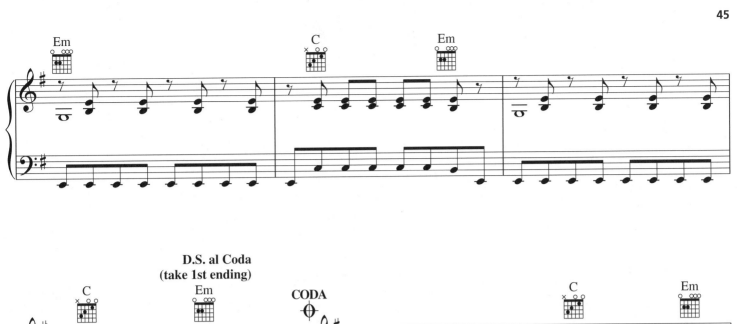

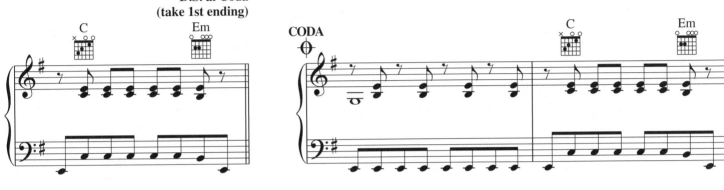

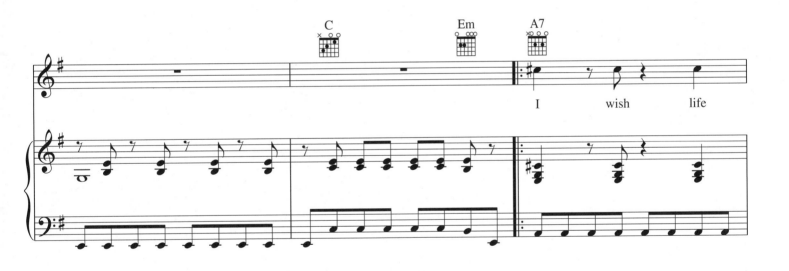

FUNTIME

Written by IGGY POP
and DAVID BOWIE

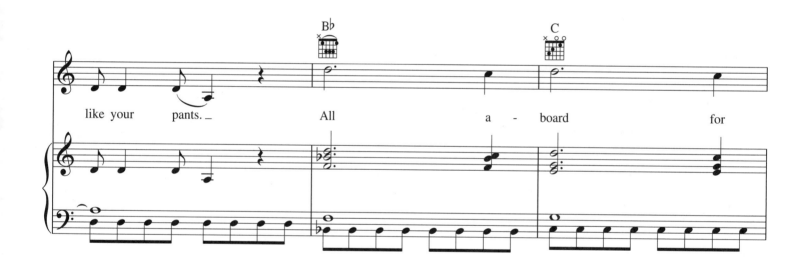

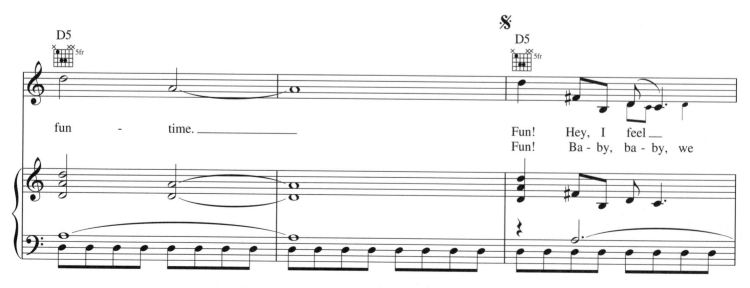

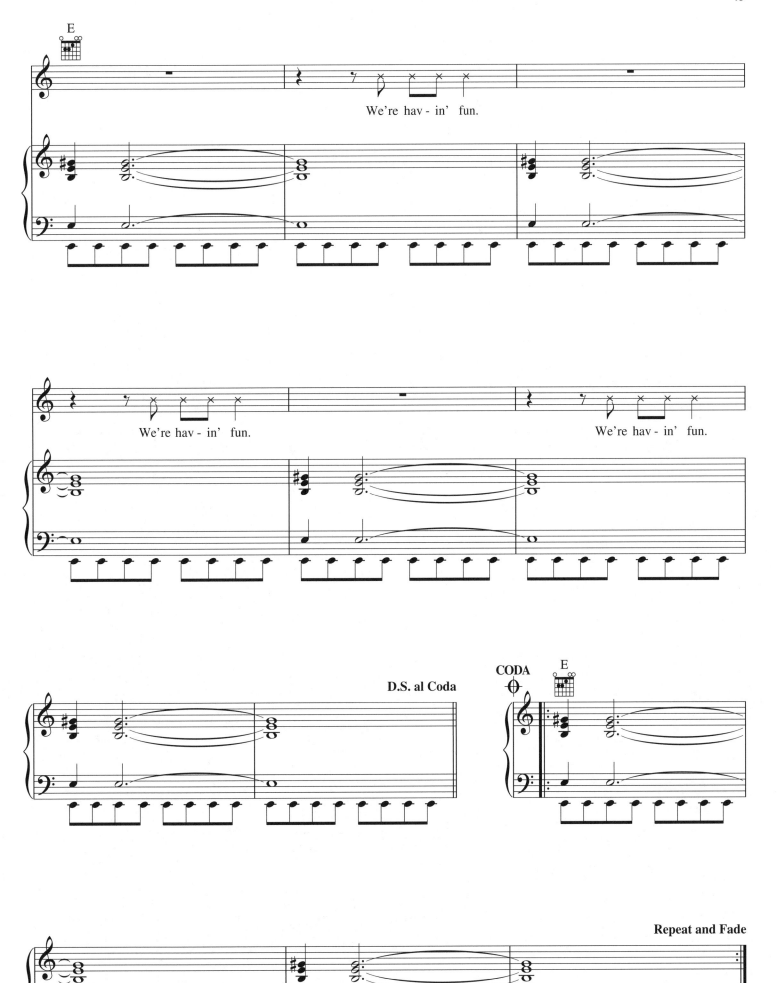

We're hav - in' fun.

We're hav - in' fun.

We're hav - in' fun.

D.S. al Coda

CODA

Repeat and Fade

GIMME DANGER

Written by IGGY POP
and JAMES WILLIAMSON

Recorded a half step lower.

HOME

Written by
IGGY POP

home. _

Vocal ad lib.

Play 6 times

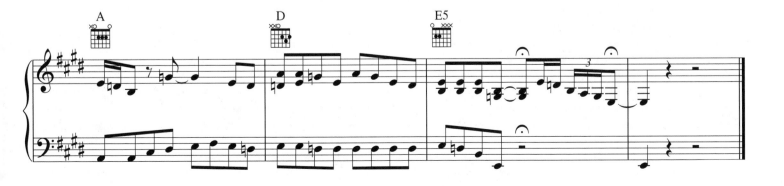

I WANNA BE YOUR DOG

Written by IGGY POP,
DAVID ALEXANDER, RONALD ASHETON
and SCOTT ASHETON

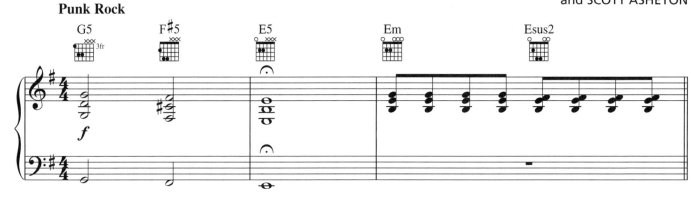

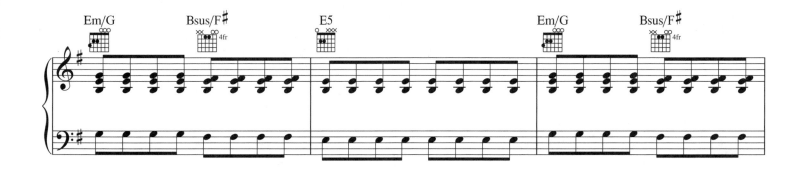

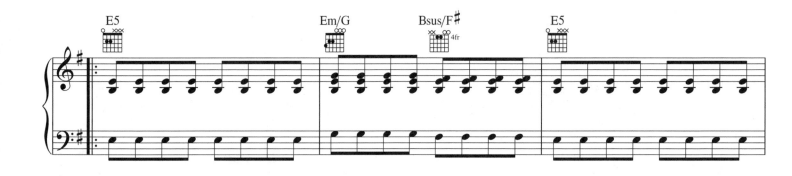

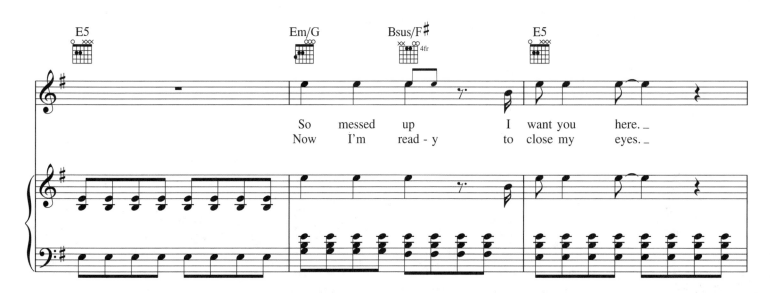

So messed up   I want you   here. _
Now I'm read-y   to close my   eyes. _

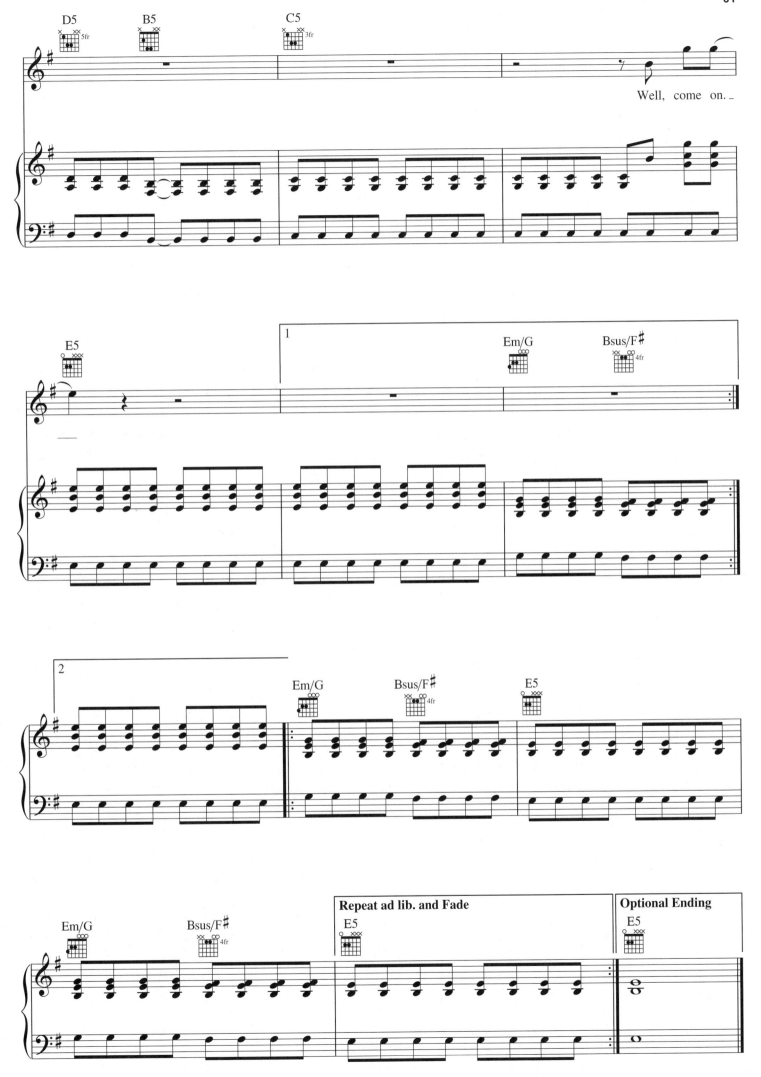

Well, come on.

LUST FOR LIFE

Written by IGGY POP
and DAVID BOWIE

THE PASSENGER

Written by IGGY POP
and RICKY GARDINER

RAW POWER

Written by IGGY POP
and JAMES WILLIAMSON

I danced to the beat of the liv-ing dead, _ Lu-cy, ba-by, stay _
Looked _ in the eyes of the sev-enth girl, _ fall deep in love in the

_ a-way from bed. _
un-der-world.

Raw pow-er is sure _ to come a-run-nin' to you. _

REAL WILD CHILD

Words and Music by JOHNNY O'KEEFE,
JOHNNY GREENAN and DAVE OWENS

SISTER MIDNIGHT

Written by IGGY POP,
DAVID BOWIE and CARLOS ALOMAR

82

D.S. al Coda

Can you hear me at all? ___

Call - ing Sis - ter Mid -

CODA

Call - ing Sis - ter Mid - night. *Guitar solo*

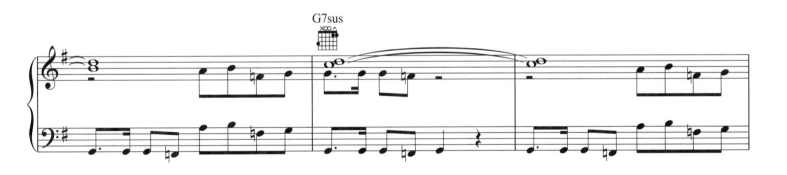

G7sus

G7   G7sus

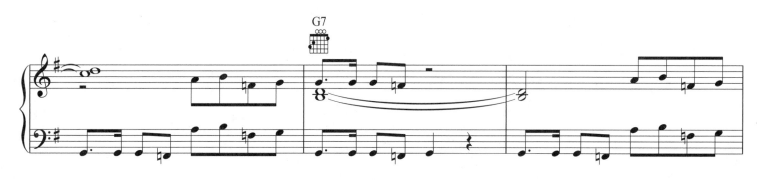

Call - ing Sis - ter Mid - night,

you know I had a dream last night.

Moth - er was in my ___ bed and I made love to her. ___

SEARCH AND DESTROY

Written by IGGY POP
and JAMES WILLIAMSON

SOME WEIRD SIN

Written by IGGY POP
and DAVID BOWIE

Moderately fast Rock

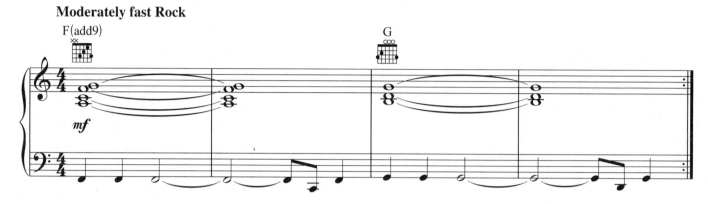

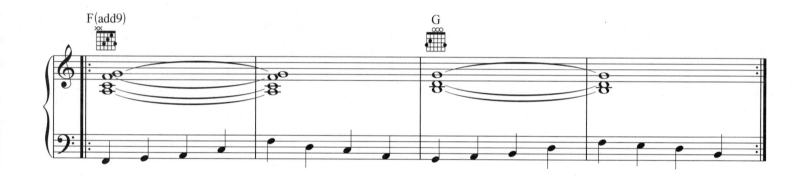

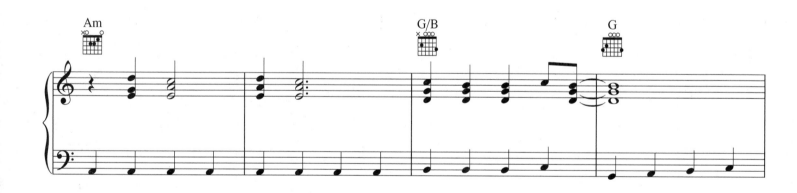

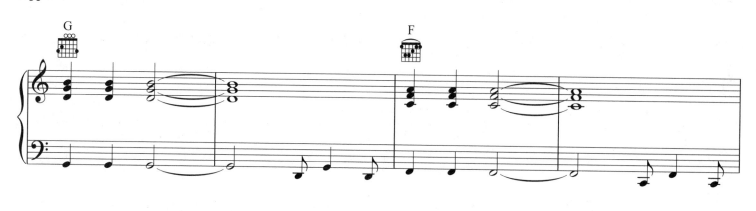

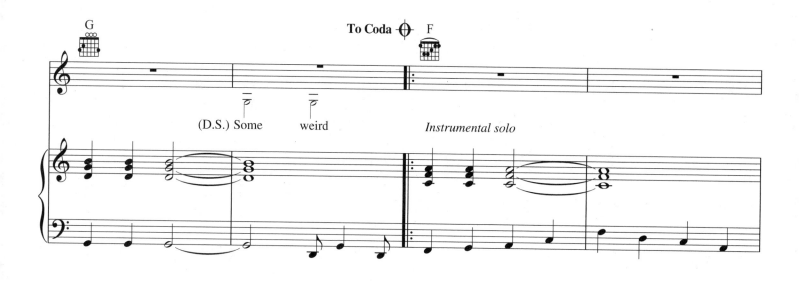

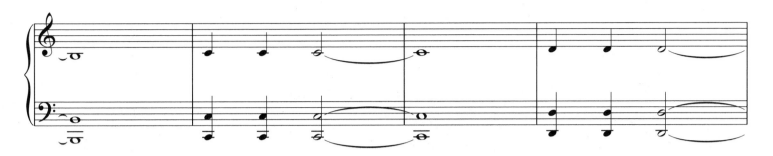

some   weird   sin. ___

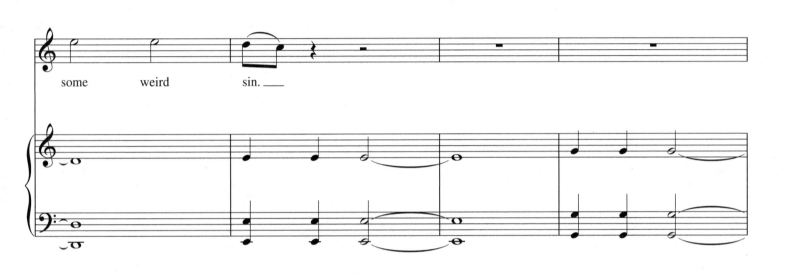

rit. poco a poco

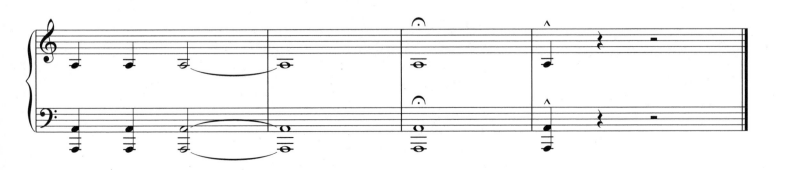

TONIGHT

Written by IGGY POP
and DAVID BOWIE

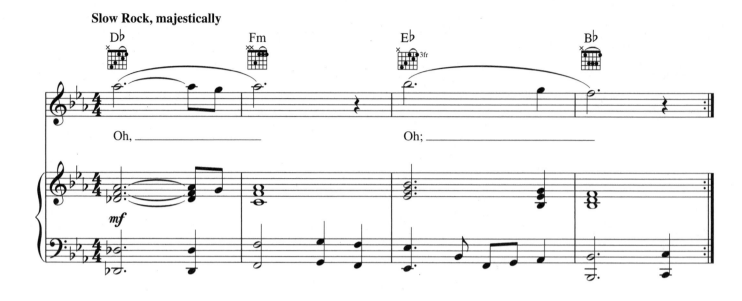

and these are the words _ to her. I said. _

Moderate Rock

Instrumental solo

- 'ry - thing _ will be al - right _ to - night. _
- 'ry - one _ will be al - right _ to - night. _
_ am goin' _ to love her till _ the end. _

Ev -